The Divorce Workbook for Children

Help for Kids to
Overcome Difficult Family Changes
& Grow Up Happy

LISA M. SCHAB, LCSW

Instant Help Books
A Division of New Harbinger Publications, Inc.

Publisher's Note

This publication is designed to provide accurate and authoritative information in regard to the subject matter covered. It is sold with the understanding that the publisher is not engaged in rendering psychological, financial, legal, or other professional services. If expert assistance or counseling is needed, the services of a competent professional should be sought.

Distributed in Canada by Raincoast Books

Copyright © 2008 by Lisa M. Schab
     Instant Help Books
     A Division of New Harbinger Publications, Inc.
     5674 Shattuck Avenue
     Oakland, CA 94609
     www.newharbinger.com

Cover design by Amy Shoup

INSTANT HELP, the Clock Logo, and NEW HARBINGER are trademarks of New Harbinger Publications, Inc.

Cover photo is a model used for illustrative purposes only.

Library of Congress Cataloging-in-Publication Data

Schab, Lisa M.
 The divorce workbook for children : activities to help kids cope with their parents' divorce / by Lisa M. Schab.
 p. cm.
 ISBN-13: 978-1-57224-601-0 (pbk. : alk. paper)
 ISBN-10: 1-57224-601-4 (pbk. : alk. paper)
 1. Children of divorced parents--Psychology. 2. Divorce--Problems, exercises, etc. I. Title.
 HQ777.5.S33 2008
 306.874--dc22
          2007051982

Printed in the United States of America

23 22 21

15 14 13 12 11 10 9

Contents

A Note To Parents

Thousands of children experience the difficulties of a divorce each year, and in spite of their parents' best intentions, divorce always has both long- and short-term effects on children. Some children, due to their personalities or other life problems, will be particularly vulnerable to the changes that accompany a divorce.

We have known for some time that there are certain things parents can do to reduce the effects of a divorce on their children. The five most important things parents can do include:

- Avoid disruptions to your children's routine.
- Don't fight with your spouse in front of your children.
- Don't criticize or blame your spouse in front of your children.
- Get professional help if you need it—don't seek comfort from your children.
- Keep your spouse involved in your child's life.

This workbook is an entirely new way you can help your child through a divorce. The activities in this workbook will teach your children the emotional and social skills they need to better cope with the divorce and be more resilient when confronted with all of life's stresses.

The activities in this workbook are very similar to the ones that a counselor would use to help children overcome the negative effects of a divorce. They will help your child express her feelings, stay out of the middle of parental disagreements, cope with change, and much more. Each activity teaches your child a new emotional intelligence skill, and once your child has learned these skills they can be applied to many other areas of life.

Children learn emotional intelligence skills just like they learn academic or athletic skills: through practice and encouragement. Your child will likely need your guidance in going through this workbook, and he or she will certainly need your encouragement.

As you help your child, you will probably find out that it is difficult for him to talk about certain issues. Never force your child to talk if he doesn't want to. The best way to get children to open up is to be a good role model. Talk about your thoughts, feelings, and experiences as they relate to each activity, stressing the positive ways that *you* cope with problems. Even if your child doesn't say a thing back, your words will have an impact on his behavior.

This workbook was designed to help any child whose parents are going through a divorce, but your child may need some additional help as well. Some children whose parents are divorcing will experience depression, anxiety, or behavior problems. If you are at all concerned about your child's reaction to your divorce, you should certainly consider consulting a trained counselor. Besides individual counseling, your child many benefit from a divorce group where children share their experiences with children of a similar age. Consult your school counselor or school psychologist to see where you can find this type of group.

If your child needs professional help—or if you need professional guidance—you will find this workbook to be of added benefit. Show it to your counselor, and she may have some additional ideas on the best way to use it.

There is no wrong way to use this workbook to help your child as long as you remain patient and respectful of your child's feelings. It can take several years for life after a divorce to seem "normal." A positive attitude will make all the difference to you and your child.

Sincerely,

Lawrence E. Shapiro, Ph.D.

Introduction

Dear Reader,

If you have been given this book, it is because your parents have gotten divorced or are planning to get divorced.

You can be sure that you are not alone in this experience. The reason this workbook was written is that a lot of children are in the same situation that you are. As you read this letter, there are children all over the country reading this same workbook and doing these same exercises because their parents have gotten divorced, too.

Divorce will bring about some changes in your life. Making these changes will be easier if you do the exercises in this book and learn ways to take care of yourself, which are called "coping skills." You will learn a number of coping skills in this book. You will also learn that there are many people in your life, including your parents, who can help you as you go through the experience of divorce. As you complete the activities, it will help if you share them with these people.

You might not be used to talking about the topics in this workbook. That's okay. As you go along, you will become more familiar with the words and ideas. And remember, there are no right or wrong answers. There are no tests or grades. All you have to do is put down the answers that are right for you, those that come from inside of you, according to your experience.

You do not have to complete every activity in this book. Some activities will be very helpful to you, but some may not have to do with your particular divorce experience. That's okay, too. Have an adult help you choose the activities that will help you the most.

Please remember to be patient with yourself as you go through the book. It can take awhile to learn something new, but you can do it! Good luck, and have fun.

Lisa M. Schab

You Need to Know

Going through a divorce can be a hard thing to do. There are a lot of things to think about, a lot of changes to make, and a lot of feelings that come up, for everyone involved. It will be easier for you to get through this experience if you remember to do two things: express your thoughts and feelings and find people to help you.

When Marcus found out his parents were getting divorced, he couldn't believe it. He had heard about divorce but he never thought it would happen in his family. For a few days, it seemed like he had just had a bad dream. He thought that if he didn't talk about it, maybe it wouldn't really be true. He thought his parents might be playing a joke on him.

But when he asked them, they said it was true. His mom would be moving out of their house and going to live with his grandparents for a while. Then his parents would go to a lawyer and sign legal papers. After that, his parents wouldn't be married anymore.

When Marcus saw his mom packing her suitcase, he realized it was true. He got very upset. He yelled at his mom and threw a pillow at her, and he ran into his room. He yelled some more and kicked his bed. Then he started crying. He didn't know what to do. He wanted to change things back to the way they used to be. He didn't want his parents to get divorced and he was afraid of all the feelings that were happening inside him.

Marcus's parents came into his room and sat beside him on the bed. They asked him to talk about what he was feeling. They said they would teach him ways to handle his feelings. They said that they would help him through the divorce, and so would his grandparents, his Scout leader and his teacher at school.

Directions

Do you remember where you were when your parents told you they were going to get divorced? Draw a picture of it here. Underneath the picture, write what your parents said and what you said.

My parents said _____

_____

_____.

I said _____

_____

_____.

More to Do

Look at the picture you drew. Write what you were thinking when it happened.

_____

_____

Write what you were feeling when it happened. _____

_____

Which of your feelings did you like? _____

_____

Which of your feelings did you not like? _____

_____

Write what you did right after you found out that your parents were getting divorced.

_____

_____

On page 1, you read about two things to do that can make it easier for you to get through your parents' divorce. Write them here:

1. _____

_____

2. _____

_____

Can you think of any other ways you can help yourself? Write them here.

_____

_____

_____

People who care about you can also help you through a hard time. Write a list of people you know who might help you handle your parents' divorce.

_____

_____

_____

_____

_____

_____

_____

_____

_____

_____

Divorce Is a Grown-Up Problem

Activity 2

You Need to Know

People get divorced for many reasons. The reasons all have to do with grown-ups and grown-up problems.

Olivia didn't understand why her parents wouldn't want to be married anymore. She didn't know what would make them get divorced and split up their family. She thought maybe it was because of something she had done.

Olivia asked her mom and dad about it when they were meeting with their counselor. "It is because there are problems between Dad and me," said Olivia's mom. But Olivia didn't know what kind of problems there could be. Her dad said they were grown-up problems. Her parents couldn't agree about how to spend their money or their time. They would argue and say hurtful things, and they couldn't seem to forgive each other. They didn't feel that they loved each other anymore, the way they had when Olivia was first born.

The counselor said people get divorced for many reasons. She made a list of some of them:

1. Sometimes grown-ups get married when they are very young—too young to know much about themselves or about the person they are marrying. As they get older, they learn that they are too different from each other to make a good couple.

2. Sometimes grown-ups hurt each other very badly. They might hurt each other by using mean words or doing mean things. The hurt is so big that they feel like they can't forgive each other, and they don't want to be together anymore.

3. Sometimes grown-ups cannot get along with each other. Everything they talk about turns into an argument. Every argument is big and lasts a long time. They argue so much that they feel bad all the time, and the rest of their family feels bad, too.

4. Sometimes grown-ups have very different ideas about how they want to live their lives. One person might want to work at their job all the time, while the other person wants to have fun all the time. One person might want to have a very big family and live on a farm, while the other person wants to have a very small family and travel from place to place.

There are other reasons that people get divorced, and they all have to do with grown-up problems and grown-up situations.

Directions

Getting divorced has to do with grown-ups and grown-up problems. The pictures below show other activities that are just for grown-ups. Write what you know about these activities.

_____

_____

_____

_____

_____

More to Do

Can you think of any other activities that are just for grown-ups? _____

_____

Why do you think these activities are just for grown-ups? _____

_____

Divorce is a grown-up problem. Can you think of any other problems grown-ups might have?

_____

_____

Why do you think these problems are just for grown-ups? _____

_____

Look back at the list that the counselor made about why people get divorced. Can you think of any other reasons people might get divorced?

_____

_____

The divorce between your parents will affect you. But remember, it is a grown-up problem that was caused by grown-ups and has to be taken care of by grown-ups.

You Need to Know

Many kids think that there was something they did, or didn't do, that caused their parents to get divorced. But that is never true. Divorce occurs because of something that happens between the adults who get divorced—not anybody else.

When Kayla's mom and dad told her they were getting divorced, Kayla thought of all the things she had done that might have made them do it. She knew they were often upset with her for not keeping her room clean. Maybe if she hadn't been so messy, they wouldn't be getting divorced. She thought about her allergies and all the times her parents had to take her to the doctor and how much they had to pay for her allergy medicine. She thought maybe if she didn't have allergies, they wouldn't be getting divorced. She remembered one time when she had missed the school bus and her mom and dad had argued about who would drive her to school. Maybe if she hadn't been late, they wouldn't be getting divorced.

Kayla felt bad about the divorce and she felt worse because she thought she might have caused it. One day her mom found her crying in her room and asked her what was wrong. When Kayla told her, she and her mom and dad had a talk. Her mom and dad explained that the divorce was about them, not about Kayla. Their problems were between the two of them and not between them and her. Their divorce had nothing to do with anything Kayla had ever done.

After their talk, Kayla felt better. She still didn't like the fact that her parents were getting divorced but at least she knew it wasn't her fault.

Directions

Did you ever think that something you did may have caused your parents' divorce?

☐ Yes   ☐ No

Draw a picture to show what you are thinking about.

Write a description that tells what is happening in your picture.

_____

_____

Tell why you think what you did may have caused your parents to get divorced.

_____

_____

More to Do

After reading this activity, do you understand that kids do not cause divorce?

☐ Yes　☐ No

If you think that you did something to cause your parents' divorce, it's very important that you talk to them about it. Share this activity with them and tell them about the picture you drew. Tell them why you think what you did may have caused them to get divorced. Then ask them if you are right.

Write their answer here.

_____

_____

_____

_____

_____

_____

_____

> ## *You Need to Know*
>
> Talking to your parents about the divorce can help you feel better inside.

When Stephen's parents first told him they were getting divorced, Stephen felt awful. He started to have a hard time falling asleep at night, and when he did sleep, he would sometimes have bad dreams. He had so many feelings inside him and so many questions that he didn't know the answers to. Would he ever see his dad again? Did his parents still love him? Was it his fault they were getting divorced?

When Stephen started getting poor grades on his homework, the teacher asked his parents to come to school. They met and talked about what was going on. They asked Stephen why he wasn't doing his homework so carefully anymore. At first, Stephen just shrugged. Then his teacher asked if something was bothering him. Stephen was kind of scared to say it but finally he did. He said the divorce was bothering him.

Stephen's parents said they hadn't known that because Stephen had never said anything. The teacher said it was time they talked. So that night at dinner, Stephen told his mom and dad everything he was feeling and asked all the questions he had. His mom and dad told him his feelings were normal, and they answered all of his questions. Stephen couldn't believe how much better he felt! His parents said he could continue telling them about his feelings and asking questions when he needed to. That night, Stephen slept deeply and peacefully.

Directions

Sometimes it's hard to put our feelings into words. It can help to use "I feel" statements. Finish the following "I feel" statements in your own words:

Mom and Dad, when you tell me you're getting divorced, I feel _____.

Mom and Dad, when I think about you getting divorced, I feel _____.

Mom and Dad, when I think about our family splitting up, I feel _____.

Are there things you would like to tell your parents or questions you would like to ask them? Paste or draw a picture of your face on the child below, and paste or draw a picture of your parents' faces on the adults. Write what you would like to tell or ask your parents. You can use "I feel" statements or your own words.

_____

_____

_____

_____

_____

_____

More to Do

Why do you think Stephen didn't talk to his parents about the divorce at first?

_____

Why do you think he then changed his mind and talked about his feelings and questions?

_____

Why do you think Stephen slept better after he had talked to his parents?

_____

Read what you wrote on page 12. Have you talked to your parents about these things yet?

☐ Yes ☐ No

If not, do you know why? ☐ Yes ☐ No

What do you think will happen if you talk to your parents about these things?

_____

If talking to your parents feels too uncomfortable, you could show them this activity or write a note telling them about your feelings and questions. Write what you would say:

Dear Mom and Dad,

_____

_____

_____

_____

_____

Love,

> ## *You Need to Know*
>
> There will be people that you want to talk to about the divorce because they help you feel better inside. There will also be people to whom you don't want to talk about the divorce, and that's okay.

Shawnna liked to talk to her grandma about her parents' divorce. Her grandma let her say whatever she wanted, and she could cry, too. Grandma was a good listener and never told Shawnna that her feelings were silly. Grandma also gave wonderful hugs.

Shawnna also liked to talk to her friend, Aimee, about the divorce. Aimee never made fun of Shawnna or thought she was dumb, no matter what Shawnna said. Aimee said she would always be Shawnna's friend.

Carson liked to talk to his school counselor, Mr. Melscher, about his parents' divorce. Mr. Melscher had an office near the principal. He always reminded Carson that whatever he said would be private, just between the two of them. Carson liked to see all the books in Mr. Melscher's office, and he felt safe there.

Carson was embarrassed at his school's Parents' Night when only his mom came with him. Some kids asked him why his dad wasn't there. He didn't want to tell them that his parents had gotten divorced and his dad had moved far away.

Directions

Circle the people below to whom you would like to talk about your parents' divorce. Put an X over those to whom you would not like to talk about your parents' divorce. Add other names to the list if you wish.

Your best friend	Your coach
Your aunt	Other friends at school
Your neighbor	Your grandparent
Your teacher	Your uncle
Your scout leader	Your counselor outside of school
Your school counselor	Your cousin
A police officer	Another child whose parents are divorced

Draw a picture of the people you would like to talk to. Write their names underneath.

_____

_____

_____

More to Do

Write each person's name that you would not want to talk to about the divorce and tell why.

_____

_____

_____

Write each person's name that you drew a picture of and tell why you would want to talk to them.

_____

_____

_____

If you were going to talk about your parents' divorce to one of these people, how would you go about asking them to listen? Write the words that you could say to ask them.

_____

_____

_____

What kinds of thoughts or feelings would you like to share with them?

_____

_____

_____

What could you say to people who ask you about your parents' divorce, if you don't want to talk about it? If you don't know what you could say, ask a grown-up for help with this question.

_____

_____

_____

You Need to Know

When your parents get divorced, there are a lot of things that change, but there are also many things that stay the same. You can help yourself feel safe and calm by remembering the things that stay the same.

When Jeremy's parents got divorced, he felt like his whole life had changed. At first it seemed like everything was different:

- His dad wasn't at his place at the dinner table anymore.

- His mom started working full-time, so Jeremy had to go to an after-school program.

- He couldn't run into his parents' bedroom to kiss them both good night.

- Instead of sleeping late on Saturday mornings, he had to get up and mow the lawn.

- There was a big, empty place in the garage where his dad's truck used to be.

Jeremy told his mom that he didn't like the way everything was changing. He felt scared and nervous. He wished that things could stay the same. His mom listened to him and said, "It might seem like everything is changing, but there are really many things that are staying the same. If you think about the things that are staying the same, you won't feel as scared or nervous." Then they sat down together at the kitchen table and made a list of all the things that were staying the same. Jeremy realized that his mom was right; if he focused on the things that were staying the same, he felt a lot better.

Directions

Here is a picture of Jeremy, surrounded by phrases that describe different things in his life. If the phrase describes something that has changed because his parents got divorced, underline it in blue. If the phrase describes something that stayed the same even though his parents got divorced, circle it in red.

Who loves him

Who his parents are

Where his dad lives

His favorite TV show

Where his dad sleeps

His favorite color

His birthday

Where he goes after school

Who his grandparents are

The color of his eyes

His favorite food

His height

His name

Where his dad parks his truck

Who his sisters and brothers are

What he does on Saturday morning

More to Do

Just like Jeremy, you have things in your life that changed when your parents got divorced and things that stayed the same.

Make a list of things that changed for you.

_____	_____
_____	_____
_____	_____

Make a list of things that stayed the same for you.

_____	_____
_____	_____
_____	_____

Did you ever feel worried about any of these changes, like Jeremy did? ☐ Yes   ☐ No

Which ones did you worry about? _____

_____

Write what you did to help yourself feel more safe and calm.

_____

_____

_____

You can make a copy of your list of things that stayed the same and put it on your mirror or in your wallet or by your bed. Remember that if you feel scared or nervous, you can help yourself feel better by thinking about all of the things that are staying the same in your life.

> ## *You Need to Know*
>
> Even if parents stop loving each other, their love for their children doesn't stop.

Molly and Evan were worried. Their parents had told them that they were getting divorced because they didn't love each other anymore. Molly and Evan wondered if their parents might stop loving them, too. They talked about their worries together. Evan thought they should ask their parents about it, but Molly was afraid to hear what their mom and dad might say.

Finally one day they did ask, and their parents told them, "VERY DEFINITELY NOT! We will never stop loving you!" Their mom and dad explained that their divorce was about the love between them. Sometimes love between parents can end. That is separate from their relationship with their children. Love between parents and children is the kind of love that never ends.

Your Parents' Love for You Doesn't Stop

Directions

There are different kinds of love, just like there are different ways to be happy or mad. Some kinds of love can change over time, but the love between parents and their child lasts forever. Solve the rebus puzzles below to find some different kinds of love. Then circle the two that will never change.

1.  2 SK+8

_____

2.

_____

3.  m+

_____

4.  2 s+

_____

5.   2 r++d m+

_____

6. m+

_____

7. m+  me

_____

More to Do

Were you ever afraid, like Molly and Evan, that your parents might stop loving you because they were getting divorced?   ☐ Yes   ☐ No

Explain your answer here. _____

_____

Make a list of some things you love right now for which your feelings might change over time.

_____   _____

_____   _____

_____   _____

_____   _____

_____   _____

Why do you think your love for these things might change? _____

_____

Why does the love between parents and their children never change? _____

_____

Do you know that your parents will never stop loving you?   ☐ Yes   ☐ No

If you answered yes, tell why. _____

_____

If you answered no, show this activity to your parents and talk to them about your fear.

Activity 8   Married or Divorced, Your Parents Take Care of You

You Need to Know

Sometimes kids are afraid that if their parents stop being married, they might also stop being parents. These kids worry that they might not have a place to live or anyone to take care of them. You need to know that it is your parents' job to continue taking care of you, even if they get divorced.

When Sierra's parents told her they were getting divorced, Sierra was scared. Her dad said he was moving out, and her mom said they couldn't afford the house anymore. Sierra wondered if they could still afford her. If her parents moved to different places, where would she live? Where would she sleep? Could she still go to school? Sierra didn't know what was going to happen.

Luckily, Sierra knew that worrying would only make her feel more scared. So she told her mom and dad all the things she was worried about, and she found out that none of her fears would come true.

Sierra's parents said that even if they were divorced, they would continue to take good care of her, just like they always had. Sierra would live with her mom during the week in a smaller house. She would live with her dad on the weekends in his apartment. She would have her own bed to sleep in at each house. She would still go to school every day, just like she always had. Her parents said they would continue to take care of her until she was grown up, just like they had always planned to.

Sierra was glad she had talked to her parents. Now she knew she didn't have to worry about having someone to take care of her.

Directions

The children in the pictures below are worried about how they will be taken care of when their parents get divorced. Color the thought balloons green if they describe worries you have had, too. Color the thought balloons red if they describe things you are not worried about.

More to Do

How did Sierra help herself feel better when she was worried? _____

_____

_____

How can the kids in the pictures help themselves feel better or get answers to their questions?

_____

_____

Write anything that you are worrying or wondering about your parents' divorce.

_____

_____

How can you help yourself feel better about these things or get your questions answered?

_____

_____

Ask your parents, or other people who can help you, to answer your questions. Write their answers here.

_____

_____

_____

Other People Who Care for You

You Need to Know

There are many other people besides your parents who can help take care of you.

Parents are usually the most important grown-ups in a child's life. They are usually the people who give the child the most and are most responsible for raising the child. But there are also other people who help to care for every child.

Many adults have jobs that involve caring for children. They might be teachers, counselors, doctors, nurses, librarians, daycare workers, social workers, or dentists. Police officers help children and so do soccer coaches, swimming instructors, and scout leaders.

Many adults care about children, even if it isn't their job. Aunts and uncles and grandparents care for their nieces and nephews and grandchildren. Neighbors can care for and help the children that live on their street. Sometimes people send money or supplies to hungry or needy children in other countries.

While your parents are probably the two people who take care of you the most, there are also other people in your life who care for and help you. These people can help you while your parents are getting divorced and even after they are divorced. You may count on them to help you at a time when your parents can't.

Some of the ways other people might take care of you include driving you where you need to go, staying with you when your parents are away, listening to you, answering your questions, playing games with you, visiting you, cooking a meal for you, helping you with your homework, teaching you a skill, taking you to the park, watching a movie with you, and watching you in a performance.

Directions

Draw or paste a picture of your face in the circle in the middle of this page. In the circles around you, draw or paste pictures of all the grown-ups who could help take care of you.

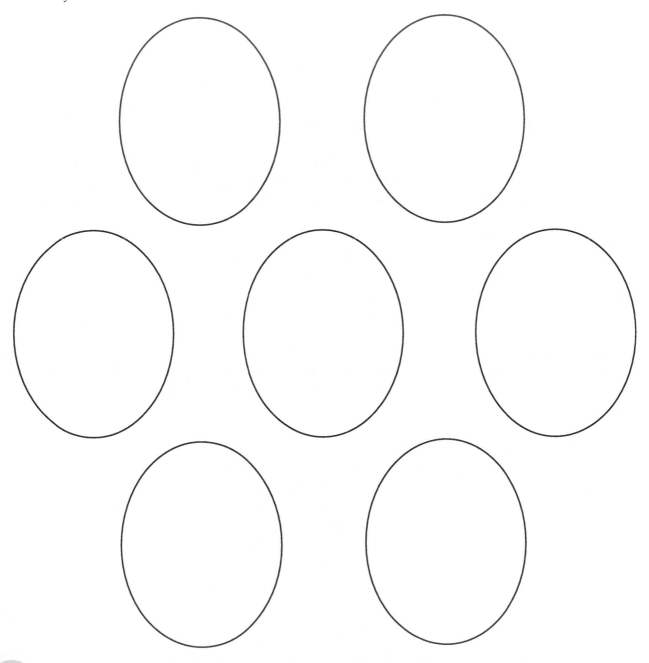

The Divorce Workbook for Children

More to Do

Write the names of the people you drew in your picture and how long you have known them.

_____

_____

_____

_____

Tell how each of these people has helped you in the past.

_____

_____

_____

_____

Tell what kinds of things each of these people could do to help to take care of you when your parents are divorced.

_____

_____

_____

_____

You Need to Know

It is normal to have a lot of different feelings when your parents get divorced. You may even have more than one feeling at a time. Expressing your feelings will help you handle them better.

When you express your feelings by talking and writing about them, you can keep them from building up inside. If you hold them in too long, you might get a headache or a stomachache or even an ache in your back.

Trying to keep your feelings inside can also make them come out at the wrong time. For example, when you are supposed to be reading out loud in class, sadness that you've held in might come out and all of a sudden you could start to cry. When your best friend accidentally bumps into you, anger that you've held in might come out and you could you push her down and hurt her.

The exercises in this book can help you express your feelings about divorce.

Directions

Under these circles are the names of feelings that some kids have when their parents get divorced. Draw in faces that show all the feelings you have had. Use the blank lines to name other feelings you have had and draw them in the circles above those lines.

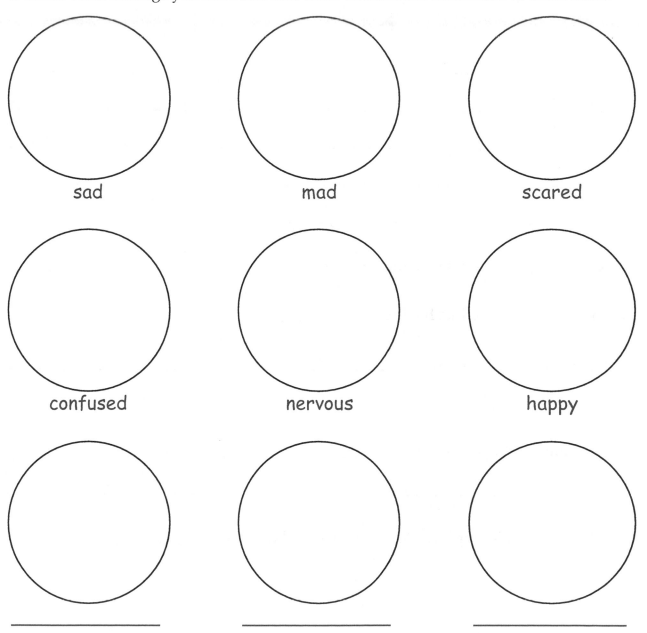

sad

mad

scared

confused

nervous

happy

_____

_____

_____

More to Do

Write each feeling that you have had and tell what made you feel that way.

_____

_____

_____

_____

_____

_____

_____

Which feeling did you like having the most? _____

Which feeling did you like having the least? _____

Which feelings did you express? _____

_____

Which feelings did you hold inside? _____

_____

Which felt better: letting your feelings out or holding them in? _____

_____

You Need to Know

When their parents get divorced, many kids feel sad.

Sadness often comes when you lose something. You might lose your favorite baseball at the park. You might lose the watch your uncle gave you. You might lose your place in line for the roller coaster. You might lose at a game you are playing. You might lose your ticket to the movies.

When your parents get divorced, you lose the way you are used to experiencing your family. You might lose living together in one house. You might lose being with both of your parents at one time. Losing these things might make you feel sad.

Directions

When people feel sad, they show it in different ways. Tell how each of the kids in these pictures is showing sadness. In the blank space, draw a picture of what you look like when you feel sad.

_____

_____

_____

_____

_____

_____

More to Do

Here are some reasons kids might feel sad when their parents get divorced:

- They might feel sad that their parents can't get along.
- When they are at their mom's house, they miss their dad.
- They won't see one of their parents as much as they used to.
- When they have to go to their mom's house, they won't be able to play with friends who live near their dad.

Is there anything about your parents' divorce that makes you feel sad? Write about it here.

_____

_____

_____

_____

_____

_____

_____

_____

Share your feelings with someone you trust. Then do the next activity to learn how to help yourself when you feel sad.

You Need to Know

You can help yourself when you feel sad by finding ways to feel comforted and doing something to forget about your sadness.

When Maria and her sisters found out that their parents were getting divorced, Maria and Elisa started to cry. Tonya just sat very still and didn't say a word. That night, the three of them sat talking on Maria's bed. They talked about how they didn't want to move, even though their parents had said they would all live in new places. They talked about how they would miss watching cartoons with their dad on Saturday mornings. They talked about how they wouldn't see their mom as much because she was going to get a full-time job. It felt like their world had fallen apart. They all hugged each other, and this time, even Tonya cried.

The next day, the girls told their Aunt Mia how sad they were. Aunt Mia said it was okay to feel sad and it was also important to find ways to help yourself when you feel sad. She said the girls could find ways to feel comforted and then they could do something that would help them forget about their sadness. That would help them get through their parents' divorce. Maria, Elisa, and Tonya made a list of things that could help them feel comforted and things they could do to forget their sadness. The next time they felt sad, instead of just thinking about all the sad things, they each asked Aunt Mia for a hug, which made them feel comforted. Then they all played cards together and forgot about their sadness for a while.

Directions

Here are some things that you can do to help yourself when you feel sad.

Things to do to feel comforted:

Cuddle with a kitten or puppy.   Ask someone for a hug.

Tell someone about your sadness.   Listen to some quiet music.

Sit on your bed under a warm blanket.

Things to do to forget about your sadness:

Play a game.   Read a happy or funny story.

Go swimming.   Ride your bike.

Watch a TV program that makes you laugh.

Circle the things above that might help you to feel better. Then write some of your own ideas.

Things I could do to feel comforted _____

Things I could do to forget my sadness _____

Draw a picture of yourself doing something to help you feel better.

More to Do

Aunt Mia suggested that the girls keep a diary to write about times they felt sad. Then they talked with Aunt Mia about what they could do in each instance to take care of themselves. Here is what they came up with.

Maria, Elisa, and Tonya's Diary

Sometimes we feel sad when we think about our family splitting apart.

> We could remind each other that the three of us will still be together. We could remind each other that our parents will still love us, even though they won't be living together. And we could help each other feel comforted by focusing on good things.

Sometimes we feel sad when we think about having to move out of the house we have lived in since we were born.

> We could take pictures of our house and make a scrapbook about it. We could write in it about all the happy times we remember here and we could take the scrapbook with us when we move. Then we could go watch TV and forget about our sadness for a while.

Sometimes we feel sad because now we will only see our dad for three days a week.

> We could talk to our dad about ways to stay in touch with him when we're not with him, like calling on the phone and sending e-mail messages. Then we could play a game with him and forget about our sadness.

Sometimes we feel sad and we're not even sure why.

> We could tell one another that we love each other. Then we could bake our favorite cookies together and tell jokes to make each other laugh.

Write about things that have made you feel sad.

_____

_____

_____

_____

_____

_____

Write what you could do to help yourself feel comforted or to forget about your sadness at each of these times.

_____

_____

_____

_____

_____

_____

You can keep your own diary at home. Just get a notebook or a journal and write in it anything you think and feel. You can share it with someone or you can keep it private, just for yourself.

You Need to Know

Many kids feel mad when their parents get divorced.

People often feel mad when they can't have something they want. You might feel mad because you want to stay up late and your parents say no. You might want to play in the park all day, but you have to go to school. You might want to have ice cream for dinner but you have to have meat loaf and peas. You might want to have your own room but you have to share with your little sister.

When your parents get divorced, you might not have everything you want. You might want them to stay married. You might want them to stop arguing. You might want things to go back the way they used to be. Not being able to have these things might make you feel mad.

Directions

When people feel mad, they show it in different ways. Tell how each of the kids in these pictures is showing anger. In the blank space, draw a picture of what you look like when you feel mad.

_____

_____

_____

_____

_____

More to Do

Here are some reasons kids might feel mad when their parents get divorced:

- They didn't want their parents to get divorced.
- Their parents made the decision without asking the kids how they felt.
- They have to move to a new house and they don't want to.
- They can't play soccer after school anymore.

Is there anything about your parents' divorce that makes you feel mad? Write about it here.

_____

_____

_____

_____

_____

_____

_____

_____

_____

_____

Share your feelings with someone you trust. Then do the next activity to learn how to help yourself when you feel mad.

How to Help Yourself When You Feel Mad

You Need to Know

You can help yourself cope with feeling mad by letting your anger out in a safe way. It is important to know the difference between actions that are safe and actions that are not safe.

When Jordan's parents got divorced, Jordan started getting into fights with kids at school. She started being disrespectful to her teacher. She always seemed to have a scowl on her face.

The school counselor talked with Jordan and helped her understand that she was mad about her parents' divorce. It was okay to feel that way, but if Jordan kept her anger inside, it might come out in ways that hurt people. Finding safe ways to let out her anger would help Jordan get through her parents' divorce. They made a list of safe things Jordan could do. The next time she felt mad, instead of picking a fight with her friend, she shot baskets into the hoop until she felt her anger going away.

Directions

Here are some ways to let your anger out safely. Put a check next to the ones you might use. On the blank lines, write some of your own ideas.

☐ Go outside and yell.

☐ Pound your fists into a pillow.

☐ Tell someone how mad you are.

☐ Go outside and bounce a ball very hard.

☐ Go outside and stamp your feet.

☐ Go outside and run around the yard.

☐ Take some very deep breaths.

☐ Cry.

_____

_____

_____

_____

Draw a picture of yourself doing something to let your anger out in a safe way.

Here are some things that you should not do to let anger out because they're not safe:

Hit someone.	Bite someone.	Kick someone.	Scratch someone.
Hurt yourself.	Hit or kick walls.	Break things.	Throw or kick things in the house.

Write some of your own ideas of unsafe things you should not do to let out your anger.

_____

_____

More to Do

Jordan's counselor suggested that she keep a diary and write down all the times she felt mad. Then they talked about what she could do in each instance to take care of herself. Here is what they came up with.

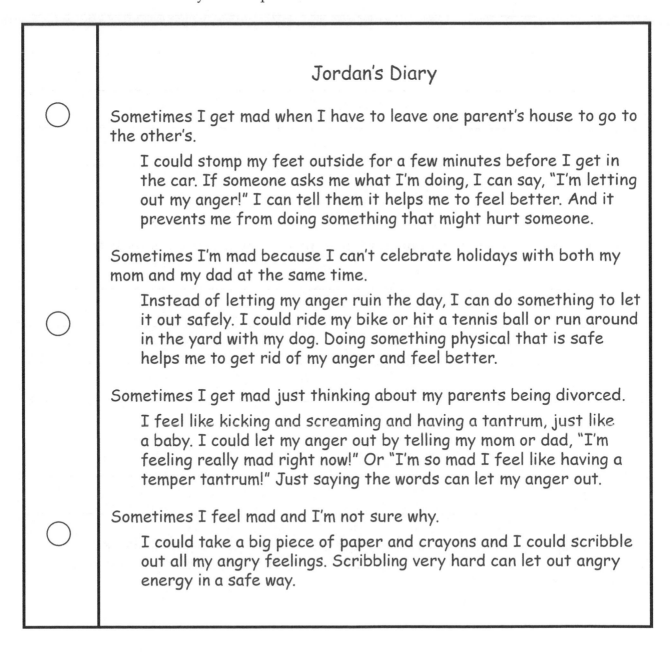

Jordan's Diary

Sometimes I get mad when I have to leave one parent's house to go to the other's.

> I could stomp my feet outside for a few minutes before I get in the car. If someone asks me what I'm doing, I can say, "I'm letting out my anger!" I can tell them it helps me to feel better. And it prevents me from doing something that might hurt someone.

Sometimes I'm mad because I can't celebrate holidays with both my mom and my dad at the same time.

> Instead of letting my anger ruin the day, I can do something to let it out safely. I could ride my bike or hit a tennis ball or run around in the yard with my dog. Doing something physical that is safe helps me to get rid of my anger and feel better.

Sometimes I get mad just thinking about my parents being divorced.

> I feel like kicking and screaming and having a tantrum, just like a baby. I could let my anger out by telling my mom or dad, "I'm feeling really mad right now!" Or "I'm so mad I feel like having a temper tantrum!" Just saying the words can let my anger out.

Sometimes I feel mad and I'm not sure why.

> I could take a big piece of paper and crayons and I could scribble out all my angry feelings. Scribbling very hard can let out angry energy in a safe way.

Write about specific things that have made you feel mad.

_____

_____

_____

_____

_____

_____

Write what you could do to let out your anger in a safe way at each of these times.

_____

_____

_____

_____

_____

_____

You can keep your own diary at home. Just get a notebook or a journal book and write in it anything you think and feel. You can share it with someone or you can keep it private, just for yourself.

Feeling Scared

You Need to Know

One common way kids feel when their parents get divorced is scared.

People often feel scared when they don't know what is going to happen or they think they might be hurt. You might feel scared if you see an older kid running toward you with a mean look on his face. You might feel scared if you learn your dad lost his job. You might feel scared if you break an expensive lamp in your house. You might feel scared if you hear about a tornado or hurricane heading for your neighborhood.

When your parents get divorced, you might feel scared because you don't know how your life is going to change. You might wonder if you will still be loved. You might not know who will take care of you if your mom has to get a job.

Directions

When people feel scared, they show it in different ways. Tell how the kids in these pictures are showing that they are scared. In the blank space, draw a picture of what you look like when you are scared.

_____

_____

_____

_____

_____

_____

More to Do

Here are some reasons kids might feel scared when their parents get divorced:

- They are scared that their parents will stop loving them.
- They are scared that they'll never see one of their parents again.
- They are scared because they don't know what divorce will be like.
- They are scared to live in a new house.

Is there anything about your parents' divorce that makes you feel scared? Write about it here.

_____

_____

_____

_____

_____

_____

_____

_____

_____

Share your feelings with someone you trust. Then do the next activity to learn how to help yourself when you feel scared.

> ## *You Need to Know*
>
> You can help yourself cope with feeling scared by asking for help and then doing something to feel safer.

After Christopher's parents told him they were getting divorced, Christopher began to have bad dreams. He would dream that he was all alone and couldn't find his parents no matter where he looked. Sometimes he dreamed that he was going to his mom's new house and he got lost and couldn't find his way. It was dark, and he was scared. Sometimes during the day he would worry about these dreams coming true, and then he couldn't concentrate on what he was doing.

The school counselor talked to Christopher and helped him to understand that he was scared about his parents' divorce. His fear was coming out in his dreams and making it hard for him to think about other things.

The counselor told Christopher it was okay to feel scared but he had to find ways to help himself. She said that Christopher could think of ways to ask for help and then do something to feel safer. That would help Christopher get through his parents' divorce. They made a list of ways to ask for help and things to do to feel safer. The next time Christopher felt scared, instead of worrying about it, he told his dad what he was afraid of. Then his dad gave him a big hug. That night he didn't have a bad dream.

Directions

Here are some things that you can do to help yourself when you are scared.

Things to do to ask for help:

Tell your mom how you feel.	Tell your dad how you feel.
Tell a teacher how you feel.	Tell a trusted grown-up how you feel.
Ask questions about what scares you.	Ask questions about things you don't understand.

Things to do to feel safer:

Sit under a warm, comfy blanket.	Ask your dad for a hug.
Ask your mom for a hug.	Go to a place in your house where you feel safe.
Stay close to a grown-up.	Hug a stuffed animal.

Circle the things above that might help you to feel better. Then write some of your own ideas.

Things I could do to ask for help _____

Things I could do to feel safer _____

Draw a picture of yourself doing something to help you when you feel scared.

How to Help Yourself When You Feel Scared

More to Do

Christopher's counselor suggested that he keep a diary and write down all of the times he felt scared. Then they talked about what he could do in each instance to take care of himself. Here is what they came up with.

Christopher's Diary

○ Since my mom and dad stopped loving each other, sometimes I'm afraid they will stop loving me too.

> I could get help by telling my mom or dad what I am thinking and asking them if it is true.

When I'm at one parent's house, sometimes I'm scared I might not see my other parent for a long time.

> I could get help by asking if I can call my other parent on the phone and find out when we will see each other again.

○ Sometimes I feel scared at night.

> I could feel safer by asking my parent to sit by my bed for a while until I fall asleep.

Sometimes I feel scared and I'm not sure why.

> I could feel safer by drawing a picture of my fear. After I draw the picture, I can rip it up!

○

The Divorce Workbook for Children

Write about the specific things that have made you feel scared.

_____

_____

_____

_____

_____

_____

Write what you could do to ask for help or to feel safer at each of these times.

_____

_____

_____

_____

_____

_____

You can keep your own diary at home. Just get a notebook or a journal book and write in it anything you think and feel. You can share it with someone or you can keep it private, just for yourself.

You Need to Know

A lot of kids feel guilty when their parents get divorced.

People often feel guilty when they think that they have done something wrong. Sometimes they really have done something wrong and sometimes they only think they have. You might feel guilty if you cheat on a test in school. You might feel guilty if you say something that hurts someone. You might feel guilty if you blame your baby brother for spilling the milk when really you spilled it yourself.

When your parents get divorced, you might feel guilty because you think that something you did or said caused their divorce. A lot of kids feel this way, but as you've learned in this book, divorce is about problems between grown-ups. It is never caused by something a child says or does.

Feeling Guilty

Directions

When people feel guilty, they show it in different ways. Tell how each of the kids in these pictures is showing that they feel guilty. In the blank space, draw a picture that shows what you look like when you feel guilty.

_____

_____

_____

_____

_____

_____

_____

_____

_____

More to Do

Here are some reasons kids might feel guilty when their parents get divorced:

- They might think their parents are getting divorced because the kids didn't always do their chores.

- They might remember a time when their parents were arguing loudly and the kids wished that one of their parents would go live somewhere else.

- They might remember that sometimes when their parents were upset with them, the kids wished they had someone else's parents.

- They might think their parents are getting divorced because sometimes they would argue about how to raise the kids.

Is there anything about your parents' divorce that makes you feel guilty? Write about it here.

_____

_____

_____

_____

_____

_____

_____

_____

Share your feelings with someone you trust. Then do the next activity to learn how to help yourself when you feel guilty.

You Need to Know

You can help yourself let go of your guilt by forgiving yourself and remembering that you did not cause your parents' divorce.

When Lizzie's parents got divorced, her little brother and her dad moved to one house, and Lizzie and her mom moved to another house. Lizzie started staying in her room a lot. When her friends called, she didn't want to talk to them. She tried to act perfect and not cause any problems at either her mom's or dad's homes. She would get frustrated, because no matter how hard she tried, she couldn't be perfect. When she got frustrated, she would cry and stay in her room.

Lizzie's mom was worried about her and took her to see a counselor. Lizzie told the counselor that she used to fight with her little brother a lot, and she thought that might have caused her parents' divorce. She said she was trying to act perfect but she could never do it right. The counselor helped Lizzie to understand that she was feeling guilty but there was no reason to. Kids can't cause their parents to get divorced—it's a problem between grown-ups.

The counselor told Lizzie it was okay to feel guilty but she had to find ways to help herself. She said that Lizzie could let go of her guilt by forgiving herself and remembering that she did not cause her parents' divorce. Doing that would help Lizzie get through her parents' divorce. They made a list of things to do to let go of her guilt. The next time Lizzie felt guilty, she forgave herself and remembered that she did not cause the divorce.

Directions

Here are some things you can do to forgive yourself and remember that you did not
cause your parents' divorce:

- ☐ Talk to someone about your feelings.

- ☐ Write yourself a kind letter, forgiving yourself for anything you are sorry you
said or did.

- ☐ Look at yourself in a mirror and smile. Say to yourself out loud, "Nothing I did
caused my parents to get divorced. Divorce is about grown-up problems."

- ☐ Instead of thinking about something you are sorry for doing, make a list of all the
good things you have done.

- ☐ Tell yourself, "Nobody is perfect. I forgive myself for doing something I'm sorry
for."

- ☐ Do Activity 3 in this book, called "Divorce Is Not Caused by Kids."

- ☐ Write yourself a reminder note that kids do not cause divorce; it's a grown-up
problem. Put the note where you will see it often.

Put a check next to the things above that might help you forgive yourself and remember
that you did not cause your parents' divorce. Then write some of your own ideas here.

_____

_____

Draw a picture of yourself doing something to forgive yourself or help you remember
that you did not cause your parents' divorce.

More to Do

Lizzie's counselor suggested that she keep a diary and write down all of the times she felt guilty. Then they talked about what she could do in each instance to take care of herself. Here is what they came up with.

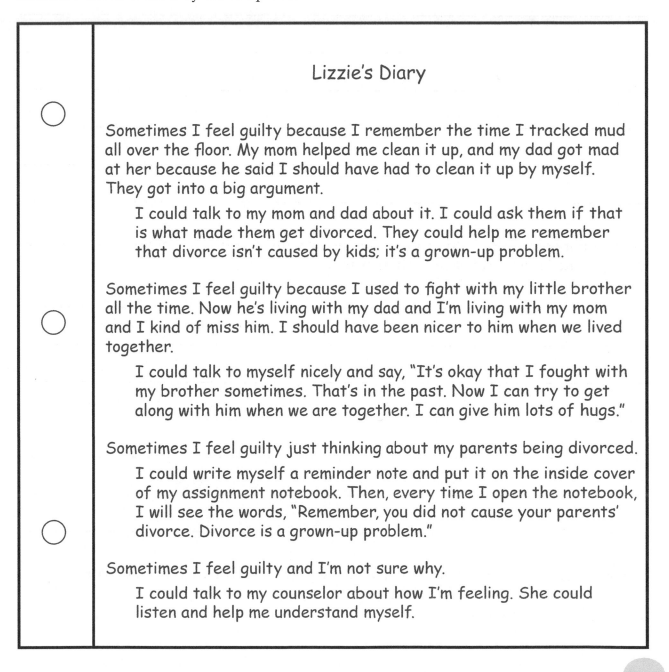

Lizzie's Diary

Sometimes I feel guilty because I remember the time I tracked mud all over the floor. My mom helped me clean it up, and my dad got mad at her because he said I should have had to clean it up by myself. They got into a big argument.

> I could talk to my mom and dad about it. I could ask them if that is what made them get divorced. They could help me remember that divorce isn't caused by kids; it's a grown-up problem.

Sometimes I feel guilty because I used to fight with my little brother all the time. Now he's living with my dad and I'm living with my mom and I kind of miss him. I should have been nicer to him when we lived together.

> I could talk to myself nicely and say, "It's okay that I fought with my brother sometimes. That's in the past. Now I can try to get along with him when we are together. I can give him lots of hugs."

Sometimes I feel guilty just thinking about my parents being divorced.

> I could write myself a reminder note and put it on the inside cover of my assignment notebook. Then, every time I open the notebook, I will see the words, "Remember, you did not cause your parents' divorce. Divorce is a grown-up problem."

Sometimes I feel guilty and I'm not sure why.

> I could talk to my counselor about how I'm feeling. She could listen and help me understand myself.

Write about the specific things that have made you feel guilty.

_____

_____

_____

_____

_____

_____

Write what you could do to forgive yourself or remind yourself that you did not cause your parents' divorce at each of these times.

_____

_____

_____

_____

_____

_____

You can keep your own diary at home. Just get a notebook or a journal book and write in it anything you think and feel. You can share it with someone or you can keep it private, just for yourself.

You Need to Know

Kids often feel helpless when their parents get divorced.

People often feel helpless when they think there is nothing they can do to change a situation. You might feel helpless if your pet is very sick and can't get better. You might feel helpless if you don't understand your homework and there is no one around to explain it to you. You might feel helpless if you see a fire and you don't know how to put it out.

When your parents get divorced, there is usually nothing that you can do to change the situation. The decision to get divorced is made by grown-ups, and kids can't change their parents' minds about it. Your mother and father will make a lot of decisions that you won't have any control over. That might make you feel helpless.

Directions

When people feel helpless, they show it in different ways. Tell how each of the kids in these pictures is showing that they feel helpless. In the blank space, draw a picture that shows what you look like when you feel helpless.

_____

_____

_____

_____

_____

_____

_____

_____

_____

More to Do

Here are some reasons kids might feel helpless when their parents get divorced:

- They can't keep their parents from getting divorced.
- They can't make their parents get along better.
- They can't keep their parents living in one house.
- They can't make their parents get back together again.

Is there anything about your parents' divorce that makes you feel helpless? Write about it here.

_____

_____

_____

_____

_____

_____

_____

_____

Share your feelings with someone you trust. Then do the next activity to learn how to help yourself when you feel helpless.

Activity 20

How to Help Yourself When You Feel Helpless

You Need to Know

You can help yourself cope with feeling helpless by telling someone who can help you and by thinking about situations where you are not helpless.

When Matt's parents told him they were getting divorced, he thought he could make them change their minds. He told them if they stayed married, he would clean the whole house every day and get straight As and give up his allowance. But they said no. Then he told them if they got divorced, he would lock himself in his room and never come out. But they didn't change their minds. Matt felt so bad, he didn't know what to do. He lay down on the floor and cried and kicked and had a tantrum, just like when he was a little baby.

After Matt's mom and dad helped him calm down, they asked him to tell them how he felt. They said it seemed like he was feeling very helpless but that he wasn't taking care of himself and his feelings were overwhelming him. Matt's mom told Matt it was okay to feel helpless but he had to find ways to help himself cope with that feeling. She said that Matt could talk more about how he felt. Then he could think about times when he did not feel helpless. They made a list of ways that Matt could tell people who could help him and ways to think about times when he did not feel helpless. The next time Matt felt helpless, he told his dad. Then he and his dad went to the park to play baseball, because baseball was something Matt was very good at. Pretty soon Matt felt confident again.

The Divorce Workbook for Children

Directions

Here are some things you can do to cope with feeling helpless.

Ways to tell someone who can help you:

- ☐ Tell your mom how you feel.
- ☐ Tell your dad how you feel.
- ☐ Tell your teacher how you feel.
- ☐ Tell your counselor how you feel.
- ☐ Tell another trusted grown-up how you feel.

Ways to think about times when you're not helpless:

- ☐ As you go through the day, notice all the times you do not feel helpless.
- ☐ Make a list of things you can do without anyone's help.
- ☐ Write a story about things you've learned to do for yourself since you were a baby.
- ☐ Make a list of things you are very smart about.
- ☐ Ask your mom and dad to help you learn new things.

Put a check next to the things above that could help you cope with feeling helpless. Then write some of your own ideas.

_____

_____

Draw a picture of yourself doing something to cope with feeling helpless.

```
┌─────────────────────────────────────────────┐
│                                             │
│                                             │
│                                             │
│                                             │
│                                             │
│                                             │
│                                             │
└─────────────────────────────────────────────┘
```

More to Do

Matt's mother suggested that he keep a diary and write down all of the times he felt helpless. Then they talked about what he could do in each instance to take care of himself. Here is what they came up with.

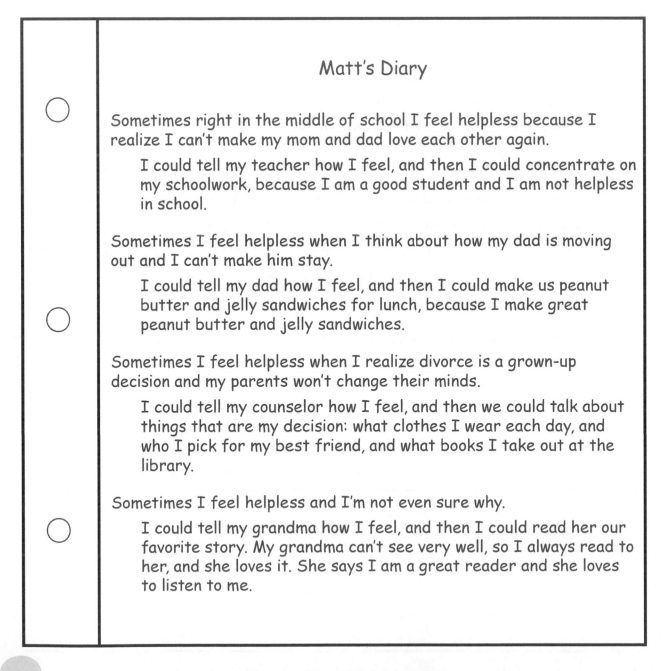

Matt's Diary

Sometimes right in the middle of school I feel helpless because I realize I can't make my mom and dad love each other again.

> I could tell my teacher how I feel, and then I could concentrate on my schoolwork, because I am a good student and I am not helpless in school.

Sometimes I feel helpless when I think about how my dad is moving out and I can't make him stay.

> I could tell my dad how I feel, and then I could make us peanut butter and jelly sandwiches for lunch, because I make great peanut butter and jelly sandwiches.

Sometimes I feel helpless when I realize divorce is a grown-up decision and my parents won't change their minds.

> I could tell my counselor how I feel, and then we could talk about things that are my decision: what clothes I wear each day, and who I pick for my best friend, and what books I take out at the library.

Sometimes I feel helpless and I'm not even sure why.

> I could tell my grandma how I feel, and then I could read her our favorite story. My grandma can't see very well, so I always read to her, and she loves it. She says I am a great reader and she loves to listen to me.

Write about the specific things that have made you feel helpless.

_____

_____

_____

_____

_____

_____

Write what you could do to cope with your feeling of helplessness at each of these times.

_____

_____

_____

_____

_____

_____

You can keep your own diary at home. Just get a notebook or a journal book and write in it anything you think and feel. You can share it with someone or you can keep it private, just for yourself.

You Need to Know

Sometimes kids feel happy when their parents get divorced.

People feel happy when situations in life turn out the way they want them to. You might feel happy when you get the present you wanted for your birthday. You might feel happy when you study hard for a test and then get a good grade. You might feel happy when you have fun at the water park.

It might sound strange to think you could feel happy when your parents get divorced. But, even if you don't like the fact that they are divorcing, there might be some things about it that turn out better and make you feel happy. It's not unusual for kids to be happy about one or two things that change.

Directions

When people feel happy, they show it in different ways. Tell how each of the kids in these pictures is showing happiness. Draw a picture of what you look like when you feel happy.

_____

_____

_____

_____

_____

_____

_____

_____

_____

More to Do

Here are some reasons kids might feel happy when their parents get divorced:

- If unhappy parents don't live together, they might not argue as much.

- If unhappy parents aren't arguing all the time, they might be easier to live with.

- Kids might get to celebrate their birthdays and holidays twice, one time with each parent.

- Kids get a break from one parent when they are visiting the other, and that might help them get along with their parents better.

Is there anything about your parents' divorce that makes you feel happy? Write about it here.

_____

_____

_____

_____

_____

_____

_____

_____

_____

Share your feelings with someone you trust.

You Need to Know

When you have feelings that are uncomfortable, you can help yourself feel better by using your thoughts.

Story 1

Carlos found out that when his parents got divorced, his mom was going to move out of their house. She was going to move into another house about a mile away. Carlos would stay with his dad for one half of the week and with his mom for the other half. Carlos listened to his parents' decision and thought:

I don't want my parents to get divorced or my mom to move out. But thank goodness, my mom isn't moving very far away; I will still get to see both my parents every week!

Carlos felt happy.

Story 2

Gina found out that when her parents got divorced, her mom was going to move out of their house. She was going to move into another house about a mile away. Gina would stay with her dad for one half of the week and with her mom for the other half. Gina listened to her parents' decision and thought:

I don't want my parents to get divorced or my mom to move out. This is awful! It will be terrible only being able to only see my mom for half of the week and my dad for half the week!

Gina felt sad and mad.

Neither Carlos nor Gina wanted their parents to get divorced. Neither of them wanted their moms to move out. But Carlos chose thoughts that made him feel happy. Gina chose thoughts that made her feel sad and mad.

Which would you choose?

Using Your Thoughts to Cope with Your Feelings

Directions

Draw a sad face above the thoughts on the left, because choosing those thoughts can make children feel bad. On the right, draw a happy face. Then, next to each thought, write a new one that can help children feel good.

I feel so sad because my parents are getting divorced. I'll never feel happy again!

_____

_____

_____

I feel so mad because my dad is moving far away and I can only see him during my summer vacation!

_____

_____

_____

I feel so scared because my parents don't love each other anymore and I think they might not love me anymore either!

_____

_____

_____

I feel guilty because last year I rode my bike into my mom's car. She got so mad. Now my parents are getting divorced, and my mom is moving away. It must be my fault.

_____

_____

_____

_____

More to Do

Look back at the stories of Carlos and Gina. The very same thing was happening to both children. Why did Carlos feel happy, but Gina felt sad and mad?

_____

_____

Why would choosing the thoughts in the right column on page 71 make kids happier than choosing the thoughts on the left?

_____

_____

What comes first inside of you: your thoughts or your feelings? _____

How can you use your thoughts to help yourself feel better? _____

_____

Write some thoughts you have had about your parents' divorce that make you feel bad.

_____

_____

_____

Now rewrite your thoughts, changing them so that they will make you feel good.

_____

_____

_____

Your thoughts are a powerful tool that you carry with you wherever you go. You can use this tool of choosing your thoughts whenever you want to feel better.

Activity 23

Using Your Body to Cope with Your Feelings

You Need to Know

When you have feelings that are uncomfortable, you can help yourself feel better by using your body.

Uncomfortable feelings can make your body feel uncomfortable, too. When you are feeling sad or guilty or helpless, your body might feel tired. When you are feeling mad or scared, your body might feel tense.

There are a number of exercises for your body that you can use to help yourself feel better.

Directions

Read over the following exercises and try each of them once. If you aren't sure how to do them, ask a grown-up for help.

Breath Detective

This exercise can be done anywhere and anytime. All you need is your breath and your attention. Check to be sure you've got both of those and then follow these directions.

1. Close your eyes.
2. Try to find your breath. Where is it right now? In your nose? Mouth? Throat? Lungs?
3. Now be a detective and, as you breathe, follow your breath wherever it goes. You don't have to try to change it. Just pay attention to it and notice where it goes in your body.
4. If you get distracted and your mind wanders, that's okay. Just find your breath and start following it again.
5. Keep following your breath for a few minutes.

When you follow your breath like that, it will automatically start to get deeper and slower. It will also take your attention off whatever is making you uncomfortable, which will help your body relax. The longer you spend following your breath, the more you will relax.

There are some places (like at your desk in school when the teacher is talking) where it wouldn't be right to close your eyes. At those times, you can still look for your breath and follow it a little, without taking your attention away from the teacher. If you practice being a breath detective with your eyes closed, you will get better at doing it with your eyes open.

Mellow Muscles

When you are tense, your muscles can feel very tight. Keeping your muscles so tight for too long can cause you to have aches and pains in your body. To help yourself feel better, you can practice having "mellow muscles," which are the opposite of tight muscles. All you need for this exercise is your muscles, a comfortable place to sit or lie down, and your imagination.

1. Sit or lie down in a very comfortable place.

2. Close your eyes.

3. Using your imagination, picture your body changing. Instead of being made of bones and flesh, it is now made of soft, squishy marshmallows!

4. Starting at the top of your head and going down all the way to your toes, picture every muscle in your body as soft as a marshmallow. Do this by thinking about each muscle and then letting all the energy out of it until it is completely soft and limp. Notice how loose each muscle feels before you move on to the next one.

When you are done with all your muscles, your body will feel soft and loose instead of hard and tight. Picturing mellow muscles helps your body relax.

Move It Out!

Another way to get tension out of your muscles is to move it out. When you push your muscles to move fast or hard, tension is released through your movement. You are literally moving it out of your body. For this exercise, you need your muscles and something physical that you love to do.

1. Make a list of physical activities that you really like. Choose those that use your muscles a lot. These might be things like riding your bike, skating, dancing, shooting baskets, running with your dog, or any other sport or activity.

2. Make a list of other physical ways you could use your muscles. These might be things like pounding your fists into your pillows, ripping up old newspapers, punching a punching bag, or vacuuming the house.

3. The next time your muscles are tense from feeling mad or scared, pick one of the activities from your list and do it.

Moving your tension out will help your muscles feel more relaxed. The activity you choose will also take your mind off your uncomfortable feelings. You might even have a great time doing it!

Super Stretch

Stretching your body is another way to move tension and uncomfortable feelings out, and it can be done more easily and quickly and in more places. For example, you might not be able to shoot baskets when you are sitting in the library or in the back seat of the car, but you can stretch out your muscles. For this exercise, you need your muscles and your brain, so you can make decisions.

1. When you feel uncomfortable or tense, use your brain to decide what part of your body you are feeling it in the most. If you decide that part is your legs, you will need to stretch your legs. If you decide that part is your neck, you will need to stretch your neck. If you decide that part is someplace deep inside of you, you will have to stretch the middle of your body.

2. Next you need to look around you and make sure there is nothing in the way of your stretch, like a person or object that could get hit. If the coast is clear, go on to the next step.

3. Pretend that you are Super Stretch, the longest stretcher in the world. Gently and slowly lengthen the part of your body that is uncomfortable. Stretch it out as far as it can safely go. Stretch so that it feels good, not so that it hurts.

4. As you stretch, picture all of the discomfort leaving through your stretched body part. Notice how good it feels to say goodbye to that discomfort.

Stretching lengthens your body and pushes the discomfort out. To start the day feeling good, you can do a whole-body super stretch every morning when you wake up. You can do another one every night before you get into bed to help you sleep better. You can do smaller stretches throughout the day, wherever you are.

More to Do

Number these exercises from 1 to 4, according to how much you liked them. Number 1 will be the one you liked best, and number 4 will be the one you liked the least.

_____ Breath Detective

_____ Mellow Muscles

_____ Move It Out!

_____ Super Stretch

Tell why you liked your first choice the best. _____

_____

Tell why you liked your last choice the least. _____

_____

Different people will be helped by the exercises in different ways. Some exercises might really help you feel better. Some exercises might not be much help. Tell which exercise helped you the most and why.

_____

_____

Using Your Body to Cope with Your Feelings

Write a story about yourself using your favorite exercise to help you feel better. If you need more room, use another piece of paper.

_____

_____

_____

_____

_____

_____

_____

_____

_____

_____

_____

_____

_____

_____

Activity 24   Mom's House, Dad's House

You Need to Know

When parents get divorced, they usually don't want to live together anymore. That means your dad will live in one place and your mom will live in another. And you will now have two places to live in because you will belong in both. That is a change from the way things were, and it may take a while before everyone gets used to it.

Keisha was not happy that her parents were no longer living together. She had liked it when her whole family lived in the same place. Now her dad lived in another town, and she and her mom had moved into a smaller house. Keisha missed her old house, where they had all lived together. She missed her old room where both her parents would tuck her into bed at night.

Her mom and dad told her that new things can take time to get used to, and after a while her two new houses would be more familiar. Then they would feel like home, too.

Can you remember the very first time you ever went to school? The school was a new place for you. It may have seemed very big at first, and you may not have known where everything was. But after a while it became more familiar, and you got used to it. Eventually you became comfortable there and maybe even started to like it. You will get used to your parents living in two houses in the same way.

Directions

You can help yourself become more comfortable with your mom and dad living in two houses by becoming more familiar with the places they live.

In the space below, paste or draw a picture of the outside of your mom's house.

What is the address at your mom's house? _____

What is the phone number? _____

Now, paste or draw a picture of the outside of your dad's house.

What is the address at your dad's house? _____

What is the phone number? _____

In the spaces below, draw a map of the inside of your mom's house and the inside of your dad's house. If you need to use more room, use separate pieces of paper instead. Show where each room is.

In each house:

- Draw your favorite food in the room that you eat in.
- Draw your favorite game or toy in the room that you play in.
- Draw your bed in the room that you sleep in.
- Draw a book in the room you do your homework in.
- Draw a toothbrush in the room that you brush your teeth in.
- Draw a star in your favorite room. Why is this room your favorite?

_____

_____

More to Do

Divorce may be one of the biggest changes you have had to get used to in your life, but it isn't the first. Think of other changes you have gone through and list them here. These changes could be anything, like having your bedroom painted or getting braces or starting a new grade at school.

_____   _____   _____

_____   _____   _____

Choose one of these changes and write more about it. How did you feel when it first happened? How long did it take you to get used to it? After a while, did it start to feel familiar?

_____

_____

_____

What is the best change that has ever happened in your life? Write about it here.

_____

_____

_____

Nothing is ever all bad or all good. Think of some things that are good about your parents' living in separate houses, and write those things here.

_____

_____

_____

Remember that you have gone through changes before. You have gotten used to them and even started to like the new situation. You can do the same thing with your parents' new living situations. Remember to be patient with yourself.

Different Houses, Different Rules

You Need to Know

When your mom and dad live in different places, they will each make rules for their own house. Some of the rules may be the same and some of the rules may be different. That may feel confusing at first, but soon you will start to remember which rules to follow in which house, just like you remember which rules to follow at a library and which rules to follow at a skating rink.

Katie and Sarah were confused and angry. Life was easier when their parents both lived in the same house. When their parents moved to different houses, Katie and Sarah had to remember two sets of rules. For example, at their mom's house, they had to clear their dishes from the table after they ate. At their dad's house, they didn't have to. At their mom's house, they could make as much noise as they wanted. But their dad lived in an apartment and he said it would bother the neighbors if they made too much noise, so they had to play quietly. Sometimes they got in trouble because they forgot they were at their dad's and were too noisy. Then the neighbors would bang on the wall, telling them to be quiet.

When your parents first get divorced, it will be harder to remember the rules for each house. But as time goes on, you will remember them more easily. It can help to write down the rules for each house and put the list where you can see it.

Directions

Draw or paste a picture of your mom in the frame below. Fill in the blanks about your mom's house rules. Use the lines if there are more rules to add.

Mom's House Rules

Who cooks _____   Who washes the dishes _____

Who takes out the garbage _____   Who does the laundry _____

When I take a bath _____   What time I go to bed _____

Who cleans up the toys _____   Where I can make a mess _____

Where I can't make a mess _____   Games I can play only outside _____

_____

_____

_____

_____

Draw or paste a picture of your dad in the next frame. Fill in the blanks about your dad's house rules. Use the lines if there are more rules to add.

[ ]

Dad's House Rules

Who cooks _____   Who washes the dishes _____

Who takes out the garbage _____   Who does the laundry _____

When I take a bath _____   What time I go to bed _____

Who cleans up the toys _____   Where I can make a mess _____

Where I can't make a mess _____   Games I can play only outside _____

_____

_____

_____

_____

More to Do

Sometimes kids get mad when they have to follow their parents' rules. They don't like to be told what they can and can't do. But usually they understand that there are reasons for these rules.

Write what would happen if no one followed the house rules.

_____

_____

_____

Why do think that some of the rules at your parents' houses are different?

_____

_____

_____

Why do you think that some of the rules are the same?

_____

_____

_____

Sometimes kids get mad because they feel like their parents broke some "rules" by getting divorced. Did you ever feel like that?

☐ Yes   ☐ No

Write what you feel and think about it.

_____

_____

_____

_____

_____

_____

_____

You Need to Know

When your parents live in two different places and you travel back and forth between them, there are many things to remember. You have to remember which days you go to which parent's house and what things to bring along with you. If you are organized, it is easier to remember everything.

Zack got frustrated every Friday morning before he went to school. It was hard to remember if it was a Friday that he should take the school bus home to his mom's house or if it was a Friday that his dad would pick him up to spend the weekend with him. If it was a "Mom" weekend, all he had to bring to school was his homework. If it was a "Dad" weekend, he had to remember his homework and his duffel bag, packed with all of the things he needed to spend the weekend at his dad's. Sometimes he would forget, and his parents would get mad at him or at each other. When that happened, everything felt awful.

One Friday morning when he got to school, his teacher, Mrs. Gress, asked Zack if everything was all right because he seemed to be upset. Zack told her he had thought at first it was a "Mom" weekend, so he didn't bring his duffel bag to school. Now he realized it might be a "Dad" weekend, but he couldn't remember for sure.

Mrs. Gress told Zack that she helped herself remember things by writing them down. She showed Zack the "Daily Planner" book that she always kept in her purse. It had a calendar where she wrote things she had to remember to do, like go to the grocery store. It also had a place for her to make lists of things to remember, like what to buy at the grocery store. She told Zack she would help him write things down so he could remember them, too.

Mrs. Gress helped Zack make a calendar. Zack's mom and dad wrote "Mom" on every weekend that he was to spend at his mom's house and "Dad" on every weekend or vacation day he was to spend at his dad's.

Mrs. Gress also helped Zack to make a list of things to remember to put in his duffel bag. Zack gave the list to his mom, and she covered it with plastic and attached it to the duffel bag with a small chain. Then every time Zack went to his dad's, he would look at the list on the bag and remember what to pack.

Directions

Use the calendar below to mark the days and times that you live at your mom's house and the days and times that you live at your dad's house this month. If you need help, ask your parents or another grown-up who knows your schedule. You can copy this calendar and make a new one each month. You can keep one copy at each house.

Month _____						

On the notebook page below, write a list of things you need to remember to bring to your mom's or your dad's house whenever you go there. These might be your homework, your toothbrush, a change of clothes, toys, or anything else you have to remember to pack. Have your parents remind you of everything you need so the list is complete. When you are done, make a copy of this page, cut out your list, and cover it with plastic, like Zack did. Then keep it in a place where you can see it whenever you have to pack.

More to Do

How do you think Zack felt when he couldn't remember if it was a "Dad" weekend or a "Mom" weekend?

_____

How do you think he felt when Mrs. Gress helped him to get organized?

_____

Is it usually easy for you to remember things or is it hard? _____

If you are upset, it can be even harder to remember everything. Are you ever upset when you have to go to visit your mom or dad?

☐ Yes   ☐ No

Tell why or why not.

_____

_____

_____

Getting organized is a big job and can take some time. Once you get organized, it will be easier to remember everything. It is important to be patient with yourself. If you make a mistake, you can always try again.

You Need to Know

When your parents are divorced, you may find that one of the hardest times is transition time—when you leave one parent's house to go to the other's. It is normal to feel some sadness at this time. You can learn how to make this time easier.

At Bryan's school, there was a special group for kids whose parents were divorced. The group met every Monday morning for one hour. A counselor led the group and helped the kids talk about what it was like when your parents were divorced.

One Monday morning, Bryan said that he'd had a crummy weekend. When his mom came to pick him up from his dad's house, he and his dad were right in the middle of playing softball. He didn't want to stop playing and he was upset. Kurt said that his parents always got into fights when they picked him up and dropped him off, and that made him feel bad. Mindy said she always felt so sad when she had to leave her mom's house, it made her cry.

Since transition time seemed to be a hard time for everyone, the counselor asked the children to think about what they could do to make it easier. They talked about it together and realized there were two steps to making transition time better. The first step was to recognize and deal with their sadness. The second step was to do something to take their mind off of it. They made a list of the ways they could do this.

How We Can Deal with Our Sadness

1. When we go to one parent's house, we can take a picture of the other parent with us.

2. When we leave one parent's house, we can write down the day and time we'll be coming back.

3. We can take the phone numbers for both houses with us, so if we start to miss our other parent, we can call to talk.

4. When we leave one parent's house, we can give them a special handshake and hug. It can be our own sign language that means, "Love you lots—See you soon!"

5. We can ask our parents to tell us again about how they still love us, even though they're divorced.

6. When we leave one parent's house to go to the other's, we can take something with us to hold onto until we get back. It might be a favorite toy or a special gift our parent gave us or a note they wrote us or something they let us borrow.

7. We can cry a little and let our feelings come out through our tears.

How We Can Forget About Our Sadness

1. While we're driving from one house to the other, we can tell our parent about the best thing that happened to us since we were last together.

2. We can bring a favorite book in the car with us and look at the pictures or read the story.

3. We can play the "Alphabet Game" in the car while we're going from one house to the other. (For this game, you look out the car window and try to find something that starts with each letter of the alphabet, like an airplane, bird, car, dog, and so on.)

4. We can play the "License Plate Game" in the car. (For this game, you look at the license plates of the cars you are passing and see how many different states you can find. Write them down to keep track.)

5. We can remember the funniest movie we have ever seen and tell the story of the part that made us laugh the hardest.

6. We can play the "See Something New Game" in the car. (For this game, you look out the window and try to find something that you have never seen before. It might be a new building, a person, an animal, or anything else.)

7. We can think about a particular game we want to play when we get home or something else fun that we are looking forward to doing.

Directions

Look at the list of ideas that Bryan's group wrote down. Circle any of the ideas that you think might help you.

Make up your own special handshake and hug that you can share with your parents when you leave them. Describe it here.

_____

_____

_____

_____

Make up a fun game that you could play while you are going from one parent's house to the other's. Describe it here.

_____

_____

_____

_____

_____

_____

_____

_____

_____

More to Do

Some kids say that transition time is hard for these reasons:

- It reminds you that your parents are divorced. (Otherwise you wouldn't have to be going from one house to the other.)
- Sometimes parents get in arguments when they see each other.
- It is hard to leave because you will miss the parent you are leaving.
- You may forget some of your things at one parent's house and have to wait until the next week to get them again.

Along with leaving your parent, you also have to leave your friends who live in that neighborhood.

Put a star next to any of these reasons that are true for you. Then write your own reasons here.

_____

_____

_____

Do your parents know that transition time can be a hard time?   ☐ Yes   ☐ No

If they don't know, how could you tell them? _____

_____

_____

You can write your list of things to do to make transition time easier. Keep copies in your mom's and dad's cars or in the bag that you pack to visit your other parent.

You Need to Know

It is normal for you to feel upset, uncomfortable, or even scared when your parents argue. You can learn to take care of yourself and help yourself feel better at these times.

Eric's parents don't argue as much as they used to, now that they are divorced and live in separate homes. But sometimes when his mom picks him up at his dad's house, they get into arguments and yell and scream at each other. Eric says it feels awful when they do that. He feels scared and sad and he wishes they would stop.

Eric's counselor told him about a game he could play that would help him when his parents argued. It was called TAG. Eric said he had played tag before with his friends. They would run after each other and try to touch the other person. When they tagged someone, they would call out, "You're It!" The person who was It always had to try tagging the other players.

The counselor said that kind of tag is lots of fun, but there is another game called TAG. This game was made up especially to help kids when their parents argue. Once Eric learned the game, he was able to take better care of himself when he heard his parents yell.

Directions

The letters in the word "TAG" tell you what to do when your parents are arguing. They stand for:

T – Tell your parents how you feel when you hear or see them argue.

A – Ask them to please stop. If they won't stop …

G – Go somewhere else, away from them, where you can't hear the argument.

The pictures below tell a story of how Eric played TAG to help himself when his parents were arguing in front of him. Number the pictures from 1 to 9 so that they tell the story in the right order.

More to Do

Have you ever heard your parents argue?   ☐ Yes   ☐ No

If you answered yes, write about one time when it happened. Tell how you felt.

_____

_____

_____

Did you ever try to stop your parents from arguing?   ☐ Yes   ☐ No

What did you try? _____

Did it work?   ☐ Yes   ☐ No

Pretend your parents are arguing now and you are going to play TAG.

Write what you would say when you **T**ell them how you feel.

_____

_____

Write what you would say when you **A**sk them to stop.

_____

_____

Tell where you could **G**o so you couldn't hear them arguing.

_____

_____

Remember that when parents argue, it is a problem between them and it is not your fault. Even if they are arguing *about* you, they are the ones deciding to have an argument. They also have to decide when to stop.

Activity 29   Caught in the Middle

Last Wednesday, Sam's mom was an hour late to pick him up. His dad got mad and told Sam that his mom was an irresponsible loser. Then he said, "Don't tell her I said that, or she might stop paying your child support." And then he said, "Oh, and don't tell her we bought a new TV either, or I'll never hear the end of it. Just tell her Grandma gave it to us."

Sam hates being put in the middle of his parents' problems. He loves them both and doesn't want to hear bad things or keep secrets or tell lies to either of them. He wishes they would keep him out of their relationship but he doesn't know how to make them stop.

Sam's parents may not realize they are hurting him by their actions. Sam can let them know by putting his feelings into words.

Directions

Choose one of these balloons to show what each child could say. Write its number in the empty balloons below.

1 — I feel hurt when you put me in the middle of an argument. Please don't use me as a messenger.

2 — I feel guilty when you put me in the middle of your secrets. Please don't ask me to lie for you.

3 — I feel sad when you criticize each other. Please don't ask me to take sides.

Tell your dad he'd better start picking you up on time!

Tell your mother I'm sick of her complaining!

You'd rather stay with me, wouldn't you?

You'd rather stay with me, wouldn't you?

Don't tell your dad that we're taking this vacation.

Don't tell your mom that I'm dating Sylvia.

Your dad took you to the movies before you finished your homework? He's so irresponsible.

Your mother drives me crazy; I never should have married her in the first place.

If your dad doesn't shape up, he's not seeing you for a month. I bet you wouldn't mind that, would you?

If your mother doesn't stop complaining, she can forget about getting any more child support from me. You know I'm right, don't you?

Your dad thinks I only make half as much money as I really do. But that's just between you and me, okay?

Your mom doesn't like it when I drink beer around you, so you won't tell her, right?

More to Do

Reread the story on page 97 about Sam. How do you think he felt when his father said those things?

_____

_____

Do you think Sam's dad knew how he felt?   ☐ Yes   ☐ No

What could Sam have said to his dad so he would stop putting him in the middle?

_____

_____

_____

Write what your own mother and father have said, or might say, to put you in the middle.

_____

_____

_____

Write what you can say to let them know how you feel.

_____

_____

_____

If your parents put you in the middle sometimes, show them this activity and tell them how you feel.

Blaming the Divorce

You Need to Know

If you are unhappy that your parents got divorced, it can be easy to blame their divorce for anything else you are unhappy about. It might feel good to do that at first, but over time it will make you feel worse. You can't change the divorce, so unless you change your outlook, you will always be unhappy. You can help yourself feel better by learning to take responsibility for yourself.

When Megan got a bad grade on her math homework, she blamed it on her parents' divorce. She told her teacher that she was doing her homework at her dad's house and he wasn't good in math. If her parents still lived together, her mom would have been there to help her, too.

When Megan got in trouble for grabbing her sister's markers away from her, Megan blamed it on her parents' divorce. She told her mom that if they hadn't gotten divorced, she wouldn't have left her own markers at her dad's house and she wouldn't have had to take her sister's.

When Megan got into an argument with her best friend, she blamed it on her parents' divorce. She said that if her parents hadn't gotten divorced, she wouldn't feel so upset all the time and then she could be nicer to her friends.

Whenever Megan felt bad, she blamed it on her parents' divorce. She was angry with her parents a lot of the time and sad a lot of the time. She told her counselor that the divorce had made her life miserable. But her counselor said that, actually, it was Megan who was making herself miserable. As long as she blamed everything on the divorce, which she couldn't change, she would always be unhappy. The way to feel better was to start taking responsibility for herself.

Megan wasn't sure how to do that. The counselor told her it meant that when she felt bad, she would understand what she had done to cause that feeling and then she would do something to make it better. The counselor said that the more she practiced, the better she would get.

Help for Kids to Overcome Difficult Family Changes & Grow Up Happy

105

Directions

Help Megan learn how to take responsibility for herself. Answer the questions next to the pictures below.

Why do you think Megan got an F on her paper?

_____

_____

_____

What could she do differently so she doesn't get an F next time?

_____

_____

_____

Why do you think Megan got into an argument with her friend?

_____

_____

_____

What could she do differently to avoid an argument next time?

_____

_____

_____

Why do you think Megan isn't outside having fun?

_____

_____

_____

What could she do differently so she can be happy?

_____

_____

_____

Why do you think Megan isn't letting her parents hug her?

_____

_____

_____

What could she do differently so she can feel loved?

_____

_____

_____

More to Do

Why do you think Megan wanted to blame everything on her parents' divorce?

_____

_____

How did blaming everything on the divorce make her feel good? _____

_____

_____

How did blaming everything on the divorce make her feel bad? _____

_____

_____

Did you ever want to blame something on your parents' divorce?   ☐ Yes   ☐ No

If you answered yes, write about it here. Then write about how you could take responsibility for yourself instead of blaming the divorce.

_____

_____

_____

_____

_____

_____

_____

No Parent Is All Good or All Bad

You Need to Know

When parents get divorced, people may want to blame one parent for all of the problems. It's important for you to know that no parent is all bad or all good.

When Isaac's parents got divorced, he found out he wouldn't be allowed to see his father very often. Isaac's mother told him that the divorce was all his father's fault. His grandma and his aunt told him the same thing. They said that Isaac's father was a "bad apple" and that Isaac was better off without him.

Isaac asked his teacher what it meant to be a "bad apple." She said that it was a person who was no good. Isaac knew that his father had a lot of problems. He knew that sometimes he drank too much and he had been fired from a couple of jobs. When Isaac was away from his father and heard his mother and her family saying negative things about him, he started thinking of his father as a "bad apple," too. If his father was no good, that would explain why they got divorced. His father had caused all the sadness.

But then Isaac went to visit his father. They watched TV together, and his father played ball with him. He gave Isaac lots of pats on the head, saying, "That's my boy." Isaac was confused. If his father was so bad, then why was he so nice to Isaac, and why did Isaac like being with him?

Directions

Fill in the blanks on the left. Then, on the right, make a list of the things you like and the things you don't like about each item.

	Things You Like	**Things You Don't**
_____ *(your best friend)*	_____	_____
	_____	_____
	_____	_____
_____ *(your school's name)*	_____	_____
	_____	_____
	_____	_____
_____ *(your favorite hobby)*	_____	_____
	_____	_____
	_____	_____
_____ *(a game or sport you like to play)*	_____	_____
	_____	_____
	_____	_____

Now place each item on the scale below, according to what you think about it.

←———————————————————————————————————→
all bad   more bad than good   1/2 bad, 1/2 good   more good than bad   all good

More to Do

Why do you think Isaac's mother and her family blamed his father for the divorce?

_____

_____

Do you think that Isaac's father was a "bad apple"?   ☐ Yes   ☐ No
Tell why or why not.

_____

_____

Was it hard or easy to think of things that you both like and dislike about the items on your list? Tell why.

_____

_____

Write the name of a child in your school that almost everyone dislikes _____

Think very hard and write something good about that child. _____

_____

Does one of your parents think the other one is all bad or all good?   ☐ Yes   ☐ No

Write something that you think is good about each of your parents.

_____

_____

_____

_____

You Need to Know

Sometimes when parents get divorced, one parent moves very far away from the other. That means you don't get to see that parent as much as the other one, and you might miss each other a lot. There are things you can do to make this separation easier.

Crystal's dad lived so far away that she had to fly in an airplane to visit him and she couldn't see him very often. She always felt very sad when she had to leave him. Her dad said they could do something special so they wouldn't feel so far away from each other. He always made sure that Crystal had a window seat on the plane. Then, when her plane was pulling away, her dad would stand right by the terminal window and hold up his red sweatshirt so she would be able to see it. He told Crystal that whenever she saw that sweatshirt it was a reminder that he loved her. And whenever she saw anything red, anywhere, she should remember that her dad was thinking about her and loved her, even when they weren't together.

Her dad's story about his sweatshirt and the color red gave Crystal a special way to feel close to him even when he wasn't there. Every time she saw something red which was almost every day, she was reminded of how much her dad loved her.

There are other ways to feel close to your faraway parent and to keep in touch, too.

Directions

Look at the kids in the pictures below. Tell how they are staying close to their faraway parents.

_____

_____

_____

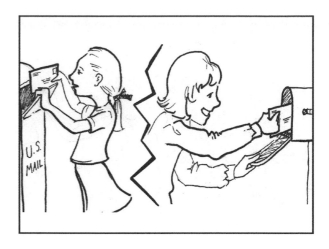

_____

_____

_____

_____

_____

_____

_____

_____

_____

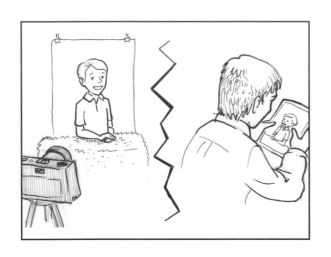

_____

_____

_____

_____

_____

_____

_____

_____

_____

_____

_____

More to Do

Do you have a parent who lives far away? ☐ Yes ☐ No

If yes, tell what it is like for you to be so far away from your parent. _____

_____

_____

Tell how often you can visit. _____

Tell what you do between visits to stay close to each other. _____

_____

_____

Look back at the pictures of the children and their parents. Circle any pictures that show something else you could do to stay close to your faraway parent. Which of these activities would you like the most?

_____

_____

Can you think of a special sign or signal like Crystal had with her dad's red sweatshirt that you could have with your parent? Describe it here.

_____

_____

_____

_____

You Need to Know

You have already learned in this book that your parents' divorce is not your fault, that the problems they have are between them, and that they will love you no matter what happens in their relationship. Sometimes, however, parents may be so upset by divorce that their sadness affects their children. Even though they love their children very much, these parents may treat them badly.

Hannah's parents had been divorced for six months, and Hannah was finally getting used to it. She was part of an afterschool group called "Rainbows" that helped kids talk about their feelings about their parents' divorce. Rainbows was helping Hannah heal her sadness.

Hannah's mom, however, didn't seem to be getting used to the divorce at all. At first she and Hannah cried a lot together. But as Hannah started feeling better, her mom seemed to be crying more. Sometimes after dinner, Hannah's mom would go into her bedroom and close the door and watch TV all by herself until she fell asleep. When Hannah asked if she could come in, her mom said no and told her to do her homework. Sometimes she yelled at Hannah to just leave her alone. The next morning, her mom would hug Hannah and tell her she was sorry and that she loved her very much. But then the same thing would happen again. Eventually Hannah's mom was staying in her room almost every night, and Hannah felt lonely and scared.

Hannah tried to talk to her dad about her mom's behavior, but her dad just said he didn't want to hear about it, in a kind of angry voice. Finally Hannah decided to tell her counselor at Rainbows. The counselor asked if any other kids in the group had parents who were very sad. Three other children raised their hands. One said her father would cry sometimes and then he would drink a lot of beer. One said that her mother didn't always go to work when she was supposed to because she didn't want to get out of bed, and the girl was afraid her mom would get fired. One child said that his father was very angry and sometimes blamed him for the divorce.

The counselor explained that sometimes parents feel so hurt that they don't know how to get over it. They might need help from a doctor or a counselor. She said it was good that the kids had told her about their parents' sadness, because now she could help them. She said she would call Hannah's mom and the other parents and help them find someone who could help them feel better again.

Directions

If your mom or dad feels so bad that they need help, these are some of the things you might notice them do. Put a check next to anything you have noticed your parent do.

☐ Yell a lot

☐ Get very angry over little things

☐ Cry a lot

☐ Not want to go out with you or their friends

☐ Stay home sick a lot

☐ Not smile very much

☐ Drink too much alcohol

☐ Tell you the divorce was your fault

☐ Say mean things to you

☐ Say very mean things about your other parent

☐ Lose a lot of weight

☐ Gain a lot of weight

☐ Sleep more than they need to

These are some of the people who might be able to help them. Put a check next to those that you think your parent might get help from. If you know the person's name, write it next to the word.

☐ Doctor _____

☐ Counselor _____

☐ Friend _____

☐ Grandparent _____

☐ Aunt _____

☐ Uncle _____

☐ Teacher _____

☐ Neighbor _____

If your mom or dad needs help, you need to get help for yourself, too. You can tell someone who will help you handle it. Put a check next to any of these people who you think might help you. If you know their names, write them next to the word.

☐ Teacher _____

☐ School counselor _____

☐ School principal _____

☐ Grandparent _____

☐ Aunt _____

☐ Uncle _____

☐ Scout leader _____

☐ Neighbor _____

☐ Coach _____

☐ Adult at your place of worship _____
_____

More to Do

Look at the list of things you have noticed your parent do. Write about the times you have noticed these behaviors.

_____

_____

Write about how you feel when your parent does these things. _____

_____

Have you ever tried to get your parent to stop doing these things?   ☐ Yes   ☐ No

If yes, tell what you tried to do.

_____

_____

If your parent is so unhappy, you probably can't get them to stop these behaviors by yourself. Make a plan to talk to someone from your list who can help your parent. Tell when you will ask for help and what you will say.

_____

_____

Make a plan to talk to someone from your list who can help you. Tell when you will ask them for help and what you will say.

_____

_____

Be sure to share this information with your parents or the person who is helping you with this book or the people whose names you wrote above. This is a time when you need to ask for help, both for your parent and yourself.

You Need to Know

Sometimes, parents who get divorced can't be part of their children's lives anymore because they are so unhappy. When that happens, it is never the children's fault.

Whitney hasn't seen her mother for two years. When Whitney's mom and dad got divorced, her mom was very angry. She also cried a lot. She didn't pay much attention to Whitney. It seemed like she didn't notice anything except her own sadness. When she moved out, she gave Whitney a hug and a kiss, but she didn't say anything; she just got tears in her eyes and then left. Whitney hasn't seen her since.

One time, Whitney got a letter from her mother from very far away. Whitney saved her mom's letter and read it every night for a long time. Whenever Whitney asked her father when she would see her mother again, he just shrugged his shoulders and said, "I don't know, honey."

Whitney's counselor said that sometimes parents are so upset when they get divorced, they might try to run away from their unhappiness by going far away. The counselor said that these parents still love their children very much, but they are too upset to be parents. Whitney said that made her feel very sad, and the counselor said she understood.

Directions

Draw a picture of a parent who is so upset that they have gone far away from the child they love.

Write about why this parent is so upset. _____

_____

_____

Write about how this parent misses their child. _____

_____

_____

More to Do

Was your parent ever so unhappy that they went far away? ☐ Yes ☐ No

If your answer is yes, tell what that was like for you and how it made you feel.

_____

_____

If your parent has gone far away, write a letter to them here. Tell them anything that you would like to say.

[ ]

If your parent has gone far away, you might have a lot of different feelings about it. Look at the exercises in this book and learn how to help yourself by expressing your feelings and finding people to help you.

Activity 35

You Can't Make Your Parents Get Back Together

You Need to Know

A lot of kids dream that their parents will get back together someday. They may even think there is something they can do to make it happen. It is important for you to know that this dream rarely comes true. In almost every case, no matter how hard kids try, they can't do anything to get their parents back together.

Both Ashley and Jared had parents who were divorced. Ashley said, "I used to daydream that one day when I was at my dad's house, I would fall off my bike and hurt my leg. Then my dad would call my mom, and she would come over. While they were fixing my bike and my leg, they would realize they still love each other and they would get back together."

Jared said, "I used to daydream that one day when I was at my mom's house, she would come into my room and find me feeling very sad. She would ask me what was wrong, and I would tell her I wanted her and my dad to get back together again. She would say, 'Okay, if you are that sad, we'll get back together.'"

Neither Ashley's nor Jared's dream ever came true.

Almost all kids would like their parents to get back together, but even if you wish and hope and dream about it, you can't make it happen. It is just wishful thinking and it isn't real.

Directions

In the pairs below, one item is real and the other is just wishful thinking. Color the real items with crayon and draw a line from each of them to "The Reality Zone." Color the wishful thinking items in pencil and draw a line from each of them to "The Wish Zone."

More to Do

Have you ever wished that your parents would get back together?   ☐ Yes   ☐ No

If you answered yes, tell how you wished it would happen. _____

_____

_____

_____

_____

_____

Do you think your wish will really come true?   ☐ Yes   ☐ No

If you answered no, how does that make you feel? _____

_____

_____

_____

_____

_____

If you answered yes to the second question, show this page to each of your parents
and ask them if you are right about your answer. Talk about it with them and tell them
how you feel.

You Need to Know

It is normal for single people to go on dates. You may not think of your parents as single people because they have children. But, since they aren't married anymore, either one of them may go on a date with someone else.

Mario's mom and dad had been divorced for two years. One day, his mom came home from the gym with a goofy smile on her face. She was singing and humming to herself as she cleaned the house. Mario asked her what was wrong because she usually didn't look happy when she was cleaning. Mario's mom said that a man at the gym had asked her to go out for dinner next weekend, and she said yes. She was singing because she felt happy. She liked the man and was looking forward to having dinner with him.

Mario was furious. He felt embarrassed by the way his mom was acting. He was mad because he would have to have a babysitter when his mom went on the date. He wondered if his mom would like the man so much, she would forget about Mario. He decided to be very rude to the man when he came over. He put a scowl on his face and wouldn't say hello. But then the man asked if Mario would like to come with him and his mom to have dinner. Mario didn't know what to say. He didn't really want to go, but he didn't want them to go without him, either. He was so confused! He ran into his room and slammed the door.

Directions

Make a list of all the feelings that you think Mario was experiencing. Next to each one, tell why you think he was feeling that way.

Mario felt _____ because _____.

Mario felt _____ because _____.

Mario felt _____ because _____.

Mario felt _____ because _____.

Mario felt _____ because _____.

Mario felt _____ because _____.

Now think of two different ways that this story could end: one where Mario feels happy and one where Mario feels sad. Draw a picture of each ending in the boxes below. On the lines underneath each picture, tell what is happening.

_____   _____

_____   _____

_____   _____

More to Do

Do you think Mario has a choice as to whether he ends up happy or sad?

   ☐ Yes   ☐ No

Tell why or why not. _____

_____

If you were Mario, tell which story ending you would choose for yourself and why.

_____

_____

Has your mom or dad ever gone on a date?   ☐ Yes   ☐ No

If yes, tell what happened. _____

_____

Tell how you felt about your parent dating and why. _____

_____

Do you think kids can stop their parents from going on dates? Why or why not?

_____

_____

Should parents listen to how their kids feel about them going on dates? Why or why not?

_____

_____

Whether or not your parent has gone on a date, it could help you to talk about it now. If you're not sure how to start, Activity 4, "Talking to Your Parents About the Divorce," can help.

Activity 37   Your Parents Still Love You Even If They Start to Date

---

You Need to Know

Your mom's or dad's relationship with their dates is separate and different from their relationship with you. If your parents start to like the people they date, or even to love one of them, that does not change or take away from their love for you.

Jack and Ben were feeling bad. They were spending the weekend with their dad as usual, but something was different. Their dad had invited a woman named Susan to go fishing with them. Susan had been nice to them and she had even baked some very good brownies to bring along to the lake. But all day whenever their dad hadn't been talking to them, he had been talking and laughing with Susan. He seemed to like her a lot. Jack and Ben were worried that if their dad started liking Susan too much, he might not have time to love them anymore. What if he wanted to go fishing with Susan only and left them at home alone? Jack and Ben were scared, and they didn't know what to do.

One night their dad found Jack and Ben whispering in their room. He asked them what they were talking about. At first they didn't want to tell him, but then Ben blurted out, "It's Susan."

That night Jack and Ben and their dad talked a lot about Susan. The boys told their dad what they were afraid of, and their dad told them how he felt about Susan. He said he liked her very much. He wanted to take her fishing with them again and other places, too. He also told them that his relationship with Susan was separate and different from his relationship with them. And he said that no matter how much he liked Susan, it would never change the love he had for them—not even one little bit. Now Jack and Ben were glad they had talked to their dad about Susan.

Directions

If one of your parents has ever had a date, draw or paste a picture of your parent and their date in the first frame.

Now draw or paste a picture of you and your parent in the second frame.

Notice how each picture is separate from the other. That is just how the relationships are in real life. Your parent's relationship with their date is separate from their relationship with you. Draw a heart around the picture of you and your parent to remind you of the love your parent has for you that will never change.

Your Parents Still Love You Even If They Start to Date

More to Do

Tell how you felt when your parent went on a date and why. _____

_____

_____

_____

Tell how you feel when you look at the picture of your parent and their date and why.

_____

_____

_____

Tell how you feel when you look at the picture of you and your parent that has the heart around it.

_____

_____

_____

Tell how much your parent loves you and how you know that. _____

_____

_____

_____

If you are worried about your parent not having enough time or love for you if they are dating, show your parent this activity and talk about how you feel.

Your Mom or Dad Might Get Married Again

You Need to Know

You have one biological mother and one biological father. It doesn't matter where they live or whom they are married to—they are your parents. Nothing can ever change that.

Kristie's mom and dad had been divorced for five years. For the past two years, Kristie's mom had been dating a man named Joe. Joe was nice to Kristie, and she liked him. Joe had two kids of his own, and Kristie liked them, too. But one day Kristie's mom told her that she and Joe were going to get married, and Joe would be her stepfather. Kristie felt very upset. She already had a father that she loved, and she didn't want or need another one. She liked Joe as a friend, but she didn't want him to be her parent. Kristie told her mom she didn't want a new father and she didn't want them to get married.

Kristie's mom told her that Joe would not be her new father. Kristie was right; she already had a father she loved and didn't need another one. Joe would never try to take the place of her biological father. He would be called her stepfather. That meant that he would continue to be her friend, just like he was now, and he would also try to take care of her and help her in any way he could.

Kristie's mom said it might help Kristie to tell Joe about her feelings and what she would like their relationship to be like. But Kristie wasn't sure she wanted to say these things to Joe. One day, Joe brought up the subject himself. He asked Kristie how she felt about having him as a stepfather and he listened to her answer. He told Kristie that he would never try to replace her biological father but he would try his best to take care of her and help her in any way he could. This helped Kristie feel better. She thought it might even be fun to have a stepfather.

Directions

The drawing below is a picture of a family tree, which shows how everyone is related in one family. Fill in the names of the people in your biological family, starting with your name at the base.

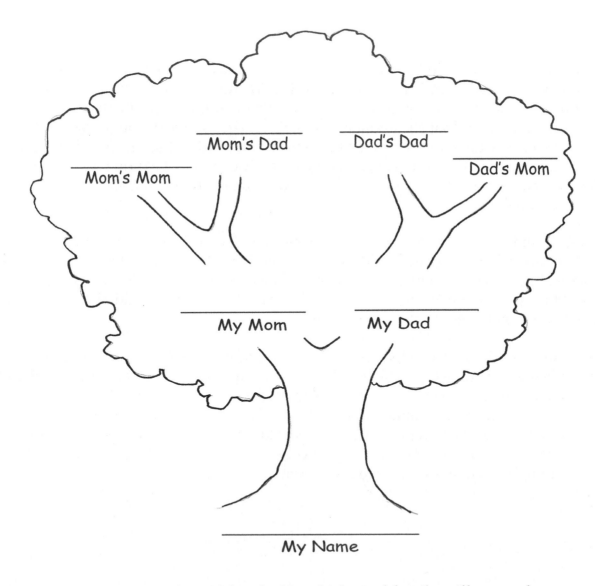

This tree shows your biological family. Your biological family will never change, even if your parents are divorced and even if they get married to someone else.

More to Do

Have you ever been in a situation like Kristie's or almost like Kristie's? ☐ Yes ☐ No

If you answered yes, tell about it here. _____

_____

What do you think you would like about your parent getting married again?

_____

_____

What do you think you would not like about your parent getting married again?

_____

_____

What kinds of questions would you like to ask someone who was going to be your new stepparent?

_____

_____

What would you like to tell that person?

_____

_____

If you haven't talked to your parent about these things, show them this activity and talk to them about your thoughts and feelings.

Activity 39　An Ending and a Beginning

You Need to Know

Just because you have come to the end of this book doesn't mean that you are done learning about how to cope with your parents' divorce. You will continue to learn ways to take care of yourself every day.

When your parents get divorced, it is the end of things the way they once were. But it is also the beginning of new things. It may be the end of the way your family used to be, but it is the beginning of the way your family will be from now on.

If you have completed the activities in this book, you have learned a lot about how to cope with your parents' divorce. As the days go on, however, you will be faced with new circumstances and new situations. Those will be times when you will learn more and grow in your ability to take care of yourself.

Directions

On the left side of this page, make a list of things that have ended in your life. On the right side, write what began because of that ending. For example, when you were very little, you stopped crawling—that was an ending. Then you started walking—that was a beginning. When you finished kindergarten, that was an ending. When you started first grade, that was a beginning.

Things That Ended	Things That Began
_____	_____
_____	_____
_____	_____
_____	_____
_____	_____
_____	_____
_____	_____
_____	_____
_____	_____
_____	_____
_____	_____
_____	_____

More to Do

Look at the list you made of endings and beginnings. You learned a lot with every ending and every new beginning. Write about some of the things you have learned.

_____

_____

_____

_____

Now think ahead to endings and beginnings that are still coming in your life. Write them here.

_____

_____

_____

_____

What might you learn from endings and beginnings that are in your future?

_____

_____

_____

Tell what is the best ending and beginning that has ever happened to you.

_____

_____

You Need to Know

If you have completed any of the activities in this book, you have taken steps toward helping yourself cope with your parents' divorce. That is a big accomplishment, and you can congratulate yourself for your effort!

You can be proud of yourself for working on something that can be hard to deal with. It means that you are a strong person and you have coping skills. You deserve a reward for working so hard!

Directions

On a copy of the certificate that follows, fill in your name. Color or decorate it with crayons, paints, markers, glitter, or any way you like. Ask a grown-up to sign it for you. When you are done, put it in a frame or someplace special where you will see it often and remember what a great job you did working on the activities in this book.

This certificate is awarded to

_____

for doing such a good job
of completing the activities

in

The Divorce Workbook
for Children.

Congratulations!

Signed by _____   Dated _____

More to Do

Make a list of ten things you have learned by using this workbook.

1. _____
2. _____
3. _____
4. _____
5. _____
6. _____
7. _____
8. _____
9. _____
10. _____

What are some things that you would still like help with?

_____

_____

_____

_____

Show this activity to a grown-up so they can celebrate your success with you and they can see what you still need help with.

Lisa M. Schab, LCSW, is a licensed clinical social worker with a private counseling practice in the Chicago suburbs. She writes a monthly parenting column for Chicago Parent magazine and is the author of eight self-help books and workbooks for children and adults. Schab teaches self-help and relaxation therapy workshops for the general public and professional training courses for therapists. She received her bachelor's degree from Northwestern University and her master's degree in clinical social work from Loyola University.

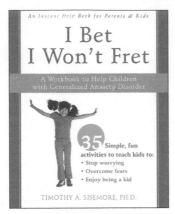